OLD FASHIONED

ISSUE

ideals

editor
Maryjane Hooper Tonn

●

managing editor
John H. Hafemeister

The hills seem wreathed
 in sunny smiles,
The trees spread leafy
 welcoming arms.
All things that beckoned
 across the miles
Display their old familiar charms.

*The landscape seems
 more lovely here,
How often in our dreams
 we yearn
To see all this that we hold dear
So sweet, so sweet
 the word return.*

Return to sunny singing hills,
To meadows we recalled
 with bliss,
Where birdsong, with bright
 rapture trills,
To home and friends
 and welcoming kiss.

© *Ruth B. Field*

IDEALS—Vol. 26, No. 3—May, 1969. Published Bimonthly by IDEALS PUBLISHING CO., 11315 Watertown Plank Road, Milwaukee, Wis. 53226. Second-class postage paid at Milwaukee, Wisconsin. Copyright © 1969 by IDEALS PUBLISHING CO. All rights reserved. Title **IDEALS** registered U.S. Patent Office.

ONE YEAR SUBSCRIPTION—six consecutive issues as published—only $7.50
TWO YEAR SUBSCRIPTION—twelve consecutive issues as published—only $14.00
SINGLE ISSUES—only $1.75

June

J. Marie Phillips

Down where the brook meanders,
Down where the wild flowers grow,
Down where the fern fronds cluster
And await the melt of snow;
Down on the hillside eager,
The mushrooms swell with pride
And crowd their leaf mold coverings
Where the flowers and trees abide.

Down where the songbirds chorus,
Down where the glades are free,
Is the wonderful place where we used
   to play,
Where there's peace and harmony.

Down where the brook meanders,
Down where the wild flowers grow,
Down where the springtime loiters,
Down where the blossoms blow.
Down where the brook meanders,
Down where the sweetest tune
Is sung by a pebble chorus
In the merry month of June.

THE OLD NEIGHBORHOOD

Mrs. Roy L. Peifer

The golden sun has gone to rest now
   in the twilight afterglow
Come, walk with me down memory lane
   to scenes we used to know.
Ah, there's the stream, the covered bridge,
   the cowpath through the wood,
And then the town, the shaded street,
   the dear old neighborhood.
The row of small white houses, each with
   its porch and swing,
The little backyard gardens where the lilacs
   bloomed in spring.
The neat white picket fences, the maple trees
   for shade,
The wide sidewalks and cool green lawns
   where children laughed and played.

The schoolhouse on the corner, the church
   with steeple high,
With its cross-agleaming landmark silhouetted
   in the sky.
'Twas just a simple little street, where folks
   were kind and good
And all of us were first-name friends in
   that old neighborhood.
The men were kindly, helpful, too; the children
   played together,
All helped to bear each other's cross,
   the storms of life to weather.
Oh, the homes may have been shabby and in
   need of some repair
But the folks behind the curtains were
   the kind of folks who care.
When sickness came to one house, anytime
   of night or day
Would other mothers from their work slip
   quietly away
To help in any way they could or bear
   some special treat
To a darkened home somewhere beside that
   friendly little street.

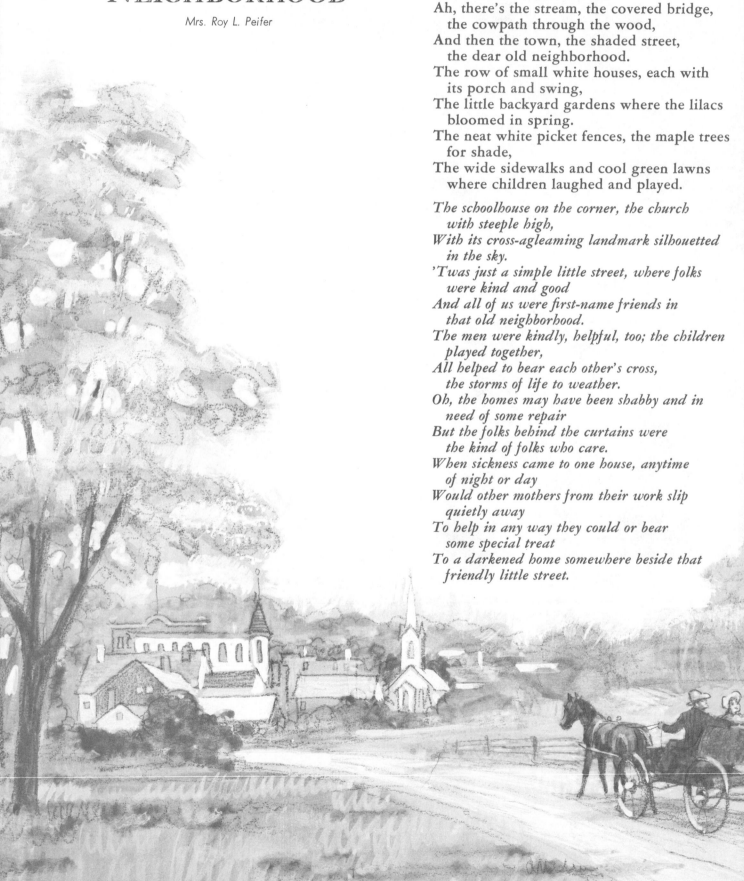

Across the back fences women traded patterns,
    recipes, bulbs and seeds;
Each shared from her oft-scant supply to fill
    another's needs.
When someone built a home, a barn, and needed
    help along the way
The neighbors rallied to his side, nor ever
    thought of pay.
No baby-sitter had we then, if care one had
    to seek,
Anyone would keep the children for an hour,
    a day, a week!
No one thought too much of getting, 'twas more
    blessed far to give,
And none were rich or famous, but all had
    learned to live.

Long years have passed but still as through
    this busy world I roam
I find my thoughts go straying to that street
    I once called home.
Could I but walk its memoried length and
    pause beside each open door
To greet my neighbors of the past in
    friendliness once more;
Or rest awhile at eventide, in someone's
    creaky swing
And listen to the children play, and hear
    the crickets sing.
Things are very different now. We travel
    such a furious pace
And knowing not the goal we seek, yet strive
    to win the race.
Life is flowing through our fingers just
    like water from a sieve . . .
We're so busy getting, spending, that we haven't
    time to live.
Oh, come my friend, a little while put all
    your cares away
And walk with me down memory lane to
    tranquil yesterday.

©

The Covered Bridge

Joy Belle Burgess

This covered bridge, quaint and weatherworn,
Still lends its dignity and charm
To the quiet little country road
That winds past meadowland and farm.
And within the stream's full melody
That echoes against its darkened walls,
It hears the tramplings of a yesteryear
Faintly above the waters' splash and fall.

And still resound the clopping hooves
Against its heavy planks;
The creaking wheels of loaded carts,
And laughter along the sun-drenched banks.
Even yet it heeds the low sweet song
Of a bygone day's rememberings,
When a swaying haycart left its drifts
And farmers tarried to talk of crops and things.

This covered bridge, quaint and weatherworn,
Still stands with dignity and charm,
Though its split and seasoned timbers
Shelter only blackbirds that fly tween field and farm.
And glints of sunlight are all that move
Across its timeworn planks . . . but still it hears
Above the waters' splash and fall,
Faint echoings of long-remembered years.

©

Rocking Chair Express

Mrs. Leon Randol

Sitting in my rocking chair
  With good books by my side,
I turn into a nomad
  And wander far and wide.

I cross the mighty ocean
  And visit Timbuktu;
Explore the ancient ruins
  Of Rome and Athens too.

Sail the streets of Venice
  With a happy gondolier,
Or call upon King Arthur
  And Lady Guinevere.

I view the Eiffel Tower,
  The pride of gay "Paree",
Or stalk the streets of Shanghai,
  So full of mystery.

The pyramids of Egypt,
  A rare sight to behold,
And the tomb of Old King Tut
  Is made of solid gold!

Thrill to all the beauty
  In this old land of ours,
Birds of brilliant color
  And wild exotic flowers.

In just a little while,
  Without train or plane or ships,
I have the wonders of the world
  At my fingertips.

Yes, through the magic of a book
  I'm a millionaire,
Travel all around the world
  And never leave my chair.

©

Hankering For Home

Evelyn Preston McLean

The world is wide and beautiful,
   Yet ever when I roam,
Before too long I wearily
   Start hankering for home.

The Taj Mahal and London Bridge,
   Pisa's Leaning Tower,
The Champs Elysee, Grand Canal,
   Enthrall me, for an hour.

The dikes of Holland, Norway's fjords,
   The Seven Hills of Rome,
Hold no allure like lofty pines
   Upon the hills of home.

Give me my homeland's lakes and streams;
   Her many charms display,
Before my homesick, lonesome eyes
   When I am far away.

The ringing of cathedral bells
   In no way can compare
With a meadowlark, sweetly singing,
   On the fence rail, over there

Behind my house at sundown,
   Nor any castle dome
Is fairer than my cottage roof,
   When hankering for home.

©

So Red the Rose

Edna Greene Hines

So red the rose
I found in beauty blooming—
So sweet its fragrance filling all the air;
So beautiful the garden all about me
It seemed, indeed, that God was walking there.

So pure the notes
I heard from treetops rising,
A matin song ascending on the air;
There was no single spot unfilled with beauty,
It seemed there was no grace it did not wear.

So clear a bell
I heard in accents pealing
As evensong rang out the day to close:
And in my heart I heard, "So close is God,
So sweet birdsongs at eve, so red the rose."

©

Remember is a lovely word,
And telescopes the years
When sliding on time's avenue
Memory appears,
To bring to life for inner eyes
The pages of the past,
Where tears and joys have merged
    to form
Rainbows that will last.

Little Red Depot

Linnea H. Bodman

Little red depot, asleep in the sun,
Your duties are over, your work is
    all done.
No longer do passengers wait at your door
And doze on your benches, or pace your
    wood floor.

*Your waiting room's cluttered with dirt
    and dead leaves,
And last season's bird's nests still cling
    to your eaves.
The track by your platform is hidden
    in grass,
And nobody gives you a glance as
    they pass.*

But your broken-paned windows remember
    the day
When life was exciting and busy and gay,
And folks in the village would gather
    to spend
A few minutes watching the train round
    the bend
And chug to a stop with a clang and
    a choke,
And a spray of its steam and a puff
    of its smoke.

*And your rusted old stove can remember
    and boast
That folks crowded round it to get warm
    as toast.
And the water tank, faded and warped
    by the sun,
Can be proud of its function to help
    the train run.*

Now all that is left are the echoes
    and sighs
Of the happy reunions and mournful good-byes.
But, little red depot, it's time now
    to rest.
Enjoy your retirement . . . you've given
    your best.

Life Is a Book

Zelda Davis Howard

Life is a book made up of days,
    Each one of us writes one.
It's opened when we come to earth
    And closed when life is done.

No pen but ours ere touches it,
    In our own way we write;
Whether we fail or we succeed
    Turns with the page at night.

And there is no erasing it
    To add or take away;
The yesterday's account is closed,
    Sealed in a white or gray.

The morning gives another sheet
    That's broad and very white,
And oh, how glorious to have
    Another chance to write!

No bad is there too small to show,
    No good that's ever lost.
All that we do goes into life's book,
    In black and white embossed.

©

Straight Shooters

Robert Edwin Anderson

"Let's pitch a game of horseshoe!"
Calls my neighbor now and then.
He seems to know my chores are done
And I'm ready to begin.

We hurry toward the backyard,
Take our "pair" and "go to court";
Ever since we were young men,
This game has been our sport.

Perhaps some rules are different now,
But the object's still the same;
When you aim better than your rival
You generally win the game.

We always aim at shooting straight,
For a level pitch and true;
We two, close friends since boys of eight,
Know they are life's rules, too.

Such fun-packed hours as these go fast,
While friendships true are made;
Soon from our minds the scores have passed . . .
Important things have stayed.

©

Where Did You Go?

Lucille McBroom Crumley

I try to think, I don't know when
She slipped away from me...
That roly-poly, curlyhead
I cradled on my knee.

It seems just overnight it came...
How could it so soon be?
She is no longer a little child,
But woman grown not yet is she.

I'd like somehow to turn back time
To that enchanted dream-filled land,
And see her playing paper dolls
Or making pies of mud and sand.

Somewhere my baby slipped away
And in her place there stands
A lovely, eager, wide-eyed girl...
My world in her two hands.

I think you must have reached up high
And plucked the stars right from the sky.
They're shining in your lovely eyes
Like little questions of surprise.

With fingers cool, the glowing dawn
Dropped on your lips the gift of song . . .
You caught from sunshine warm and bright
Your radiant smile to give delight.

A breath of fragrance in the air
Brushed dusk of evening in your hair.
A little elf so sweet and gay,
You danced into my heart to stay.

©Ona Jane Meens

Miracle

Sweeter than the violets of spring
And a deeper mystery by far
Than all the other lovely blooms
And more than Heaven's brightest star . . .
This miracle is you, my child,
I kiss your precious little face
And know I'll never understand
This miracle that God has wrought.
Yet the proof is quite enough.
Just to hold your hand in mine
Is to know a miracle divine.

Grace Mathews Walker

I would not give you wealth to show,
For it's in seeking that we grow.
But, best of all, I would impart
The giving joy of a loving heart.

©Evelyn Stanley

Scherenschnitte
by Walter von Gunten

The Smaller Joys

Edgar A. Guest

Give me the simple joys: the wild
    bird's song,
A rose or two to cherish as my own,
A dwelling small where constant love
    is known.
And I'll not murmur that life's way
    is long.

Give me a sheltering tree, a patch
    of lawn,
A few good friends to share my
    merry hours,
To walk with me and bend above
    my flowers
And I'll rejoice to greet the
    coming dawn.

Give me some tasks to do,
    not leadership,
Nor brilliant effort with its
    larger gain,
But tasks which serve a need
    and soften pain
And I can face the world with
    smiling lip.

Give me this small success: to play
    the friend,
To hold my post with courage,
    and to be
Free from the chains of pomp
    and luxury
And I can walk, glad-hearted, to
    the end.

Picture opposite
KILBOURN HOUSE
Milwaukee, Wisconsin

Arbor Day

Minnie Klemme

He who plants a tree plants more than shade . . .
A landmark yet within the glade;
A place where children climb and swing,
A place where birds may nest and sing;
A place where stars peek through the leaves,
Where raindrops glide and tall winds grieve,
Where God from far-off, golden skies
May pause at times to rest His eyes.

*He who takes a spade and plants a tree
Can look beyond infinity,
For as the tree grows limb by limb,
Man, too, can reach out arms to Him
Who gave the tree the will to grow . . .
So plant a tree and you will know.*

©

A Growing Tree

Leonard G. Nattkemper

I never see a little tree
But wonder what its life will be;
What trials and triumphs it will meet
In winter's cold and summer's heat.

*I always hope that it will find
A life worth living, sweet and kind;
That it will love the changing sky
And welcome seasons passing by.*

That it will sweetly join in song
And motion when the winds are strong;
And in the flowering time of spring
Will nest the mating birds that sing.

*I hope if woodmen cut it down,
They'll build of it a home in town
Where love abides and children play,
And parents teach them how to pray.*

I do so love a little tree,
For God, it makes me think of Thee;
Of all Thy blessings showered on us
A growing tree's most wondrous.

©

Prayer of the Woods

A Portuguese Prayer

Ye who pass by and would raise your hand against me, hearken ere you harm me.

I am the heat of your hearth on the cold winter nights, the friendly shade screening you from the summer sun, and my fruits are refreshing draughts quenching your thirst as you journey on.

I am the beam that holds your house, the board of your table, the bed on which you lie, and the lumber that builds your boat.

I am the handle of your hoe, the door of your homestead, the wood of your cradle, and the shell of your coffin.

I am the gift of God! I am the friend of man!

Ye who pass by, listen to my prayer. Harm me not.

Trees Take Time

Patience Strong

Trees take time to grow. They can't be hurried. Slow but sure—they gain a little day by day and patiently endure the fury of the winter storms. As centuries pass by, roots go deeper as the boughs reach up into the sky.

There it stands, the massive oak, a giant in height and girth, but it was an acorn once, a small seed in the earth. And still it grows—year in year out the mighty branches climb, up and up towards the light . . . but slowly. Trees take time.

©

Golden Moments

Val Becklund

There are golden moments in each day
  That God gives for our pleasure;
They make the world a wondrous place,
  Give memories to treasure.

These moments that we hear and see
Add to our book of memory.

These golden moments are for all
  Who pause from earthly clamor
To refresh their souls with God's handiwork,
  To see the world's bright glamor.

The colors pleasing to each eye
With expert hand God does apply.

The forests green with shady paths,
  The meadows bright with sunlight;
The air resounding with birdsongs,
  Streams gurgling with delight.

God also sends great storms and showers
To prove to us His mighty powers.

The azure of the lakes reflects
  The skies on each bright day;
The sunsets flaming in the west . . .
  God's paintings on display.

The brilliance of a snowy scene,
Winter with its cold blue sheen.

Life need not be a barren path,
  Just pause each day to capture
The golden moments God has given
  To add to life sweet rapture.

Let's clear our minds so that we may
Find golden moments in each day!

©

Main Street

Craig E. Sathoff

A two-block length of little shops
Of mortar, brick, and wood
Make up the Main Street of the town
I've loved since my boyhood.

The Main Street is the very heart
Within the little town,
And though the stores aren't stately there,
They've a splendor all their own.

There is the well-stocked general store
Which boasts variety;
Huge bolts of goods and boots and shoes,
Fresh fruits, and groceries.

The barber pole, red, white, and blue,
Beside its tidy shop
Hangs o'er a bench of weathered wood
Where all are free to stop.

The blacksmith with his red-hot forge,
The dentist with his drill,
The druggist with his remedies
Are part of Main Street still.

But what I like the very best
About our small Main Street
Are smiling faces of the friends
That one is sure to meet.

©

The Country Store

W. T. Kimberl

I do a lot of reminiscing
As the evening shadows fall,
While sitting by the fireplace . . .
There the old days I recall.

*I relive the old-time moments
From my boyhood days of yore,
And in fancy I am once again
At the old-time country store.*

There the old familiar objects
Are in memory closely wove,
As again I see the cracker barrel
And the old potbellied stove.

*I can hear the village people
As they pass the time of day.
I can see the old-time "drummer"
As he goes his merry way.*

Then there's a game of checkers
With the village champion there.
You may be sure the game goes on,
Be the weather foul or fair.

*Yes, there was a lot of living
In those days of yesteryear . . .
And tonight I live them over
While I shed a silent tear.*

©

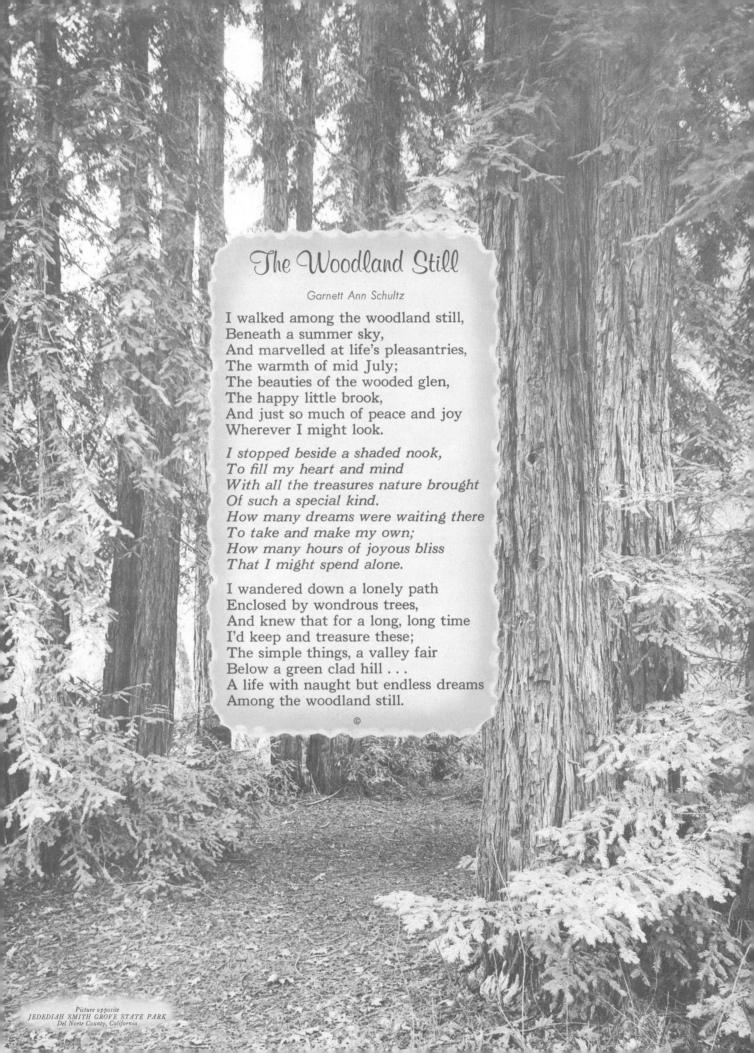

The Woodland Still

Garnett Ann Schultz

I walked among the woodland still,
Beneath a summer sky,
And marvelled at life's pleasantries,
The warmth of mid July;
The beauties of the wooded glen,
The happy little brook,
And just so much of peace and joy
Wherever I might look.

I stopped beside a shaded nook,
To fill my heart and mind
With all the treasures nature brought
Of such a special kind.
How many dreams were waiting there
To take and make my own;
How many hours of joyous bliss
That I might spend alone.

I wandered down a lonely path
Enclosed by wondrous trees,
And knew that for a long, long time
I'd keep and treasure these;
The simple things, a valley fair
Below a green clad hill . . .
A life with naught but endless dreams
Among the woodland still.

©

LOOKING EASTWARD

Mason C. Robinson

To westward of the valley deep
  I sit, face toward the east,
And there I see blue sky, white clouds,
  A green world underneath.
The summer warmth, the silver haze,
  The ripple of the leaves,
The church whose spire of purest white
  Adorns the distant hill;
These things are mine for taking time
  To pause and be quite still.

It is a Sunday afternoon,
  The day God made for man
To rest from all his worldly cares
  And look upon the land
Which God and he together have
  Fine-fashioned with their toil.
'Tis time to let contentment play
  Its part for a little while.

The world goes well around me where
  I hear the songs of birds.
Their world is surely sweet to them,
  Too sweet for tuneless words.
The warm, soft rain of yesterday
  Lends fragrance to the breeze
Which wafts so gently past me bearing
  Scents of flowers and trees.

Over the distant hill a winding road
   Invites from here beyond
The range of vision to perceive
   Or ear to gather sound.
But where it passes out of view
   Is green and pleasant land
Where dawns each day that He designs
   And quickens with His wand.

Tomorrow I shall start again
   Along life's winding road
Which as today, leads through a land
   That God and man made good.
With eye and ear, rich senses blessed
   To share in nature's wealth,
I shall be richer, more content
   With life for life itself.

I've loved to look to eastward since
   The time I was a child.
Recalling days which came from there,
   They beamed, oh! how they smiled.
And now I watch as day declines,
   The sun caress with hues
These eastern hills and tint His sign,
   "Tomorrow will be yours".

©

Homespun

Adeline Roseberg

Homespun, though a humble word,
Is rugged as a mountain ridge;
Deep as the flow of river currents,
And sturdy as a bridge.

Homespun, though a rugged word,
And stalwart as an oak,
Is graceful as a leaping deer,
And warming as a cloak.

Homespun, though a sterling word,
Is gentle as a dove;
As charming as an old-time tune,
And tender as young love.

Homespun, an enduring word,
Fraught with memories sweet to recall
Is starlit as well as down-to-earth,
And beloved by great and small.

©

MOONGLOW

Ruth G. Nelson

The moon in all its splendor rose,
Grasping in its enchanted throes
A weary, sick and darkened world,
And then its magic it unfurled.

*Drab streets were clothed in soft moonglow
As Nature staged her matchless show,
And rooftops showed off their full height
As moonbeams penetrated night.*

Tree limbs moved gently in the breeze
Like ghostly arms that sought to seize
A moon-washed and star-studded sky,
And then I heard the owl's night-cry.

*And while I stood there, still, entranced,
Even my being was enhanced
As nighttime worked its healing way,
Relieving tensions of the day.*

Thick darkness fades before its power
As moonlight woos each fleeing hour,
And lithesome shadows come to birth
As moonbeams bathe night-shrouded earth.

*Stars lending their own special light
To what has been dark lurking night
Help Nature's wondrous enterprise
Of lighting earth from distant skies.*

And so I seek to praise in verse
The wisdom of the universe
Who made nighttime part of His plan
To soothe and comfort distraught man.

©

*Scherenschnitte
by Walter von Gunten*

The Ship of Life

Dolores Mary Blessent

As a little ship we go sailing
On the sea of life.
We have much to encounter
As life presents success and strife.

How we meet each challenge
Is the test that life prepares . . .
A strong faith and true courage
Is so needed to conquer life's cares.

When our faith is faltering
  and our courage wanes
On this stormy sea of life, we seek
A guiding light to guide us
On a course now dark and bleak.

We can find this guiding light
In our Heavenly Father above.
With care so true and kind
He will gently guide us with His love.

©

They that go down to the sea in ships,
That do business in great waters;
These see the works of the Lord,
And his wonders in the deep.
Psalm 107:23, 24

Peace Will Come

Garnett Ann Schultz

Peace will come on a brighter day
When a fairer dawn shall break,
And the guns of war shall be laid aside
With the toll of lives they take.
Stars will shine in a peaceful sky
Where clouds shall be no more,
And every smile will bring happiness
Without a thought of war.

Peace will rule in a fearless world
Where right shall surely win,
And eyes will glow with a sweet content
Where doubts and tears have been.
Where once a kiss brought a longing ache
For the loved one far away,
And only a mem'ry filled the heart
Where a dear one couldn't stay.

Peace will come . . . we must never doubt,
For faith must last through all,
Though precious boys must pay the price
And heed their country's call.
We must be as sure of our victory,
For true as the setting sun,
We'll never lose if we keep the thought
That some day peace will come.

©

Famous Men

Arthur Guiterman

Forever honor those who, great of heart,
Reared up the land we love and made it strong!
God give us equal strength to do our part
As they did theirs, like them to face all wrong
Unflinchingly. As they were brave and just,
So may we prove; and yet, as time in flight
Brings other ways and better ways we trust,
May we find nobler means to aid the right
Than their day knew. God's road is all uphill
And man climbs slowly. These were fine and true,
But we must bear their banner higher still;
What else would those we honor have us do?
The past's a scroll whereon great truths are found,
But not a chain by which men's feet are bound.

IRVING BERLIN'S BUGLE SONG
OH! HOW I HATE TO GET UP
IN THE MORNING

BY
IRVING
BERLIN

"Oh! How I Hate To Get Up In the Morning"
by Irving Berlin
©Copyright 1918 Irving Berlin
©Copyright Renewed
Used by Permission of Irving Berlin Music Corporation

A Memory

Emma A. Lent

A day of tender memory,
A day of sacred hours,
Of little bands of marching men,
Of drums and flags and flowers.

A day when a great nation halts
Its mighty throbbing pace,
And by its meed of gratitude
Shows love with willing grace.

A day to keep from year to year
In memory of the dead;
Let music sound and flowers be laid
Upon each resting bed.

Memorial Day

Edgar A. Guest

Blow gently, winds of May,
And softly stir the trees,
Whispering today
The love we bear to these
Who sleep that silent sleep,
At rest forevermore.
Blow gently, winds of May . . .
Their warfare now is o'er.

Blow gently, winds of May,
Bearing the perfume rare
Of blossoms o'er the way;
Rose petals scatter there;
The starry flag we place
In glory on each grave,
Catches in a fond embrace
For us and proudly waves.

Blow gently, winds of May,
Shine softly, summer sun;
Our heroes sleep today,
Their duty nobly done.
And with the flag they loved,
And flowers, we come today
To honor those who sleep . . .
Blow gently, winds of May.

As I Go My Way

Strickland Gillilan

My life shall touch a dozen lives
Before this day is done,
Leave countless marks for good or ill
Ere sets this evening's sun.
From out each point of contact of
My life with other lives
Flows ever that which helps the one
Who for the summit strives.

Does love through every handclasp flow
In sympathy's caress?
Do those whom I have greeted know
A newborn hopefulness?
Are tolerance and charity
The keynote of my song,
As I go plodding onward with
Earth's eager anxious throng?

My life must touch a million lives
In some way, ere I go
From this world of struggle
To the land I do not know.
So this is the wish I always wish,
The prayer I ever pray . . .
Let my life help the other lives
It touches by the way.

COMPASSION

Viney Wilder

Compassion is a healing word,
It has the gentle sound
Of summer rain on leaves, wind-stirred,
Above the fertile ground.

It sheds a soft compelling glow
Where understanding thrives,
Outreaching every word we know
In touching broken lives.

And he who makes this word to live,
Through action on his part,
Shall learn that God delights to give
The warm impulsive heart.

There are loyal hearts, there are spirits brave,
There are souls that are pure and true;
Then give to the world the best you have,
And the best will come back to you.

Give love, and love to your life will flow,
A strength in your utmost need;
Have faith, and a score of hearts will show
Their faith in your work and deed.

Madeline S. Bridges
(1844–1920)

The Bridges We Build

Esther Baldwin York

How many bridges have you noticed today?
. . . Natural bridges of rock or vine or
fallen tree . . . An insect's bridge spun
of gossamer web . . . Man's bridges of
stone or wood or steel for teeming
traffic over land or water . . . Bridges
are of many kinds.

*How many bridges have you built today?
. . . Bridges of growth, of learning, of
understanding . . . Bridges of thought, of
friendship, of love . . . Bridges of faith,
of courage, of prayer . . .*

©

Build a Bridge

Dorothy Butler Kimball

If you build a wall around yourself,
How lonely you will be.
You cannot live your life that way,
At least, not happily.

*A bridge, instead, bids welcome
To the folks who would befriend.
So build a bridge, then come halfway
Towards the other end.*

©

Picture opposite
GOLDEN GATE BRIDGE
San Francisco, California

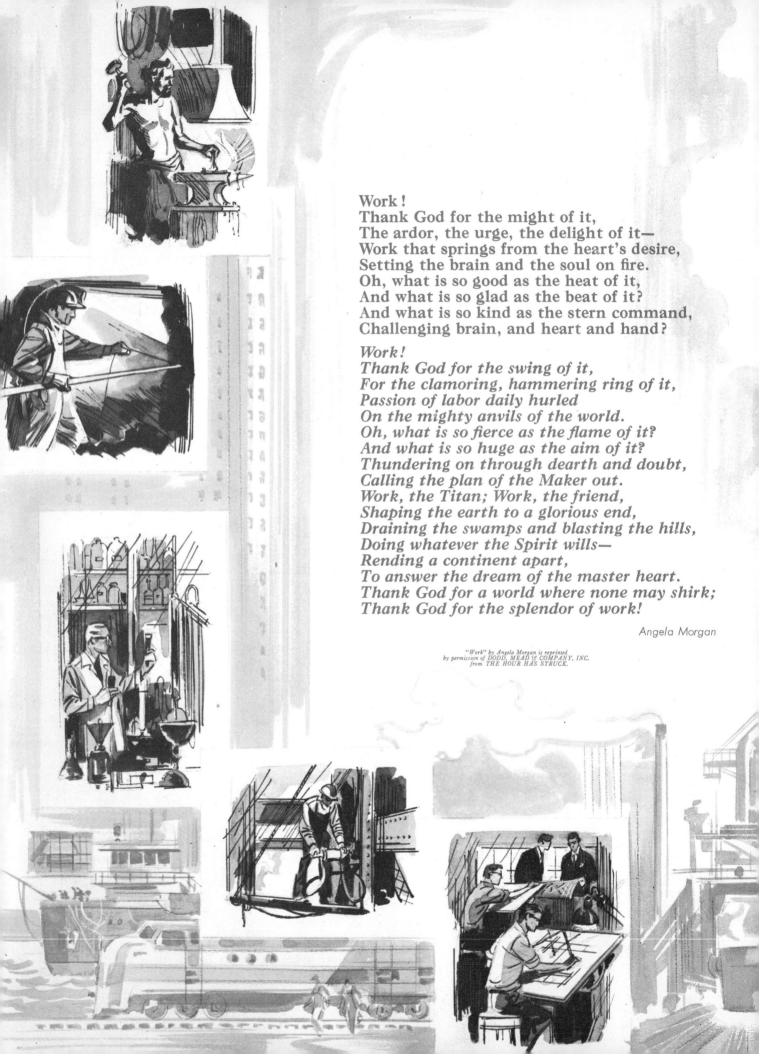

Work!
Thank God for the might of it,
The ardor, the urge, the delight of it—
Work that springs from the heart's desire,
Setting the brain and the soul on fire.
Oh, what is so good as the heat of it,
And what is so glad as the beat of it?
And what is so kind as the stern command,
Challenging brain, and heart and hand?

*Work!
Thank God for the swing of it,
For the clamoring, hammering ring of it,
Passion of labor daily hurled
On the mighty anvils of the world.
Oh, what is so fierce as the flame of it?
And what is so huge as the aim of it?
Thundering on through dearth and doubt,
Calling the plan of the Maker out.
Work, the Titan; Work, the friend,
Shaping the earth to a glorious end,
Draining the swamps and blasting the hills,
Doing whatever the Spirit wills—
Rending a continent apart,
To answer the dream of the master heart.
Thank God for a world where none may shirk;
Thank God for the splendor of work!*

Angela Morgan

"Work" by Angela Morgan is reprinted
by permission of DODD, MEAD & COMPANY, INC.
from THE HOUR HAS STRUCK.

Work

If you are poor, work.
If you are rich, continue to work.
If you are burdened with seemingly
  unfair responsibility, work.
If you are happy, keep right on working.
  Idleness gives room for doubts and fears.
If disappointments come, work.
If sorrow overwhelms you and loved ones
  seem not true, work.
If health is threatened, work.
When faith falters and reason fails, just work.
When dreams are shattered and hope seems dead,
  work as if your life were in peril.
  It really is.
Whatever happens or matters, work.
Work faithfully, work with faith.
Work is the greatest material remedy available.
Work will cure both mental and physical afflictions.

Author Unknown

Patriotism

Sir Walter Scott

Breathes there the man with soul so dead,
Who never to himself hath said,
"This is my own, my native land!"
Whose heart hath ne'er within him burned
As home his footsteps he hath turned
From wandering on a foreign strand?
If such there breathe, go, mark him well;
For him no minstrel raptures swell;
High though his titles, proud his name,
Boundless his wealth as wish can claim;
Despite those titles, power, and pelf,
The wretch, concentred all in self,
Living, shall forfeit fair renown,
And, doubly dying, shall go down
To the vile dust from whence he sprung,
Unwept, unhonored and unsung.

Ten Little Steps

Loise Pinkerton Fritz

Back to the home of my childhood days
I wandered this summer past,
To find a welcome beyond compare;
Tears of joy, reunion at last
With family and ties of yesteryear,
Like the old stairway that has . . .
    Ten little steps that lead upstairs
    Where once we said our bedtime prayers.

*In high-heeled shoes and frilly gowns
And bonnets so stylishly sewn,
We'd make believe for many an hour
That like Mother and Dad we were grown.
Time cannot erase those happy hours
We joyously played upon . . .
    Ten little steps that lead upstairs
    Where once we said our bedtime prayers.*

I'm sure no one my thoughts could mete
Nor read this heart of mine,
As once again I longed to be
A child of eight or nine,
So I could kiss dear Mom and Dad
Good night, then slowly climb . . .
    Ten little steps that lead upstairs
    And once more say my bedtime prayers.

Are All the Children In?

Author Unknown

I think oftimes as the night draws nigh
Of an old house on the hill,
Of a yard all wide and blossom-starred
Where children played at will.

And when the night at last came down,
Hushing the merry din,
Mother would look around and ask,
"Are all the children in?"

'Tis many and many a year since then,
And the old house on the hill
No longer echoes to childish feet,
And the yard is still, so still.

But I see it all, as the shadows creep,
And though many the years have been
Since then, I can still hear mother ask,
"Are all the children in?"

I wonder if when the shadows fall
On the last short, earthly day,
When we say good-bye to the world outside,
All tired with our childish play,

When we step out into the other land
Where Mother so long has been,
Will we hear her ask, just as of old,
"Are all the children in?"

Grandma's Doll

R. Phillipy

I wonder what stories she could tell,
   Grandma's painted china doll . . .
For she guards her secrets well,
   Sitting prim and proper against the wall.

She has an air of elegance
   In her pink dress trimmed with lace;
She brings a feeling of quaint romance
   And poignant mem'ries of bygone days.

She has won a favored place
   In the heart of a girl of ten,
For this doll with the painted face
   Was her confidante and friend.

Grandma's childhood toys were few,
   But this cherished china doll,
Her joy and tears and secrets knew . . .
   She knew and shared them all.

Ties, past and present, seem combined
   In the doll that Grandma left to me,
As she surveys the changing times
   With ageless grace and serenity.

©

The Children's Hour

Henry Wadsworth Longfellow

Between the dark and the daylight,
  When the night is beginning to lower,
Comes a pause in the day's occupations
  That is known as the children's hour.

I hear in the chamber above me
  The patter of little feet,
The sound of a door that is opened,
  And voices soft and sweet.

From my study I see in the lamplight,
  Descending the broad hall stair,
Grave Alice and laughing Allegra,
  And Edith with golden hair.

A whisper, and then a silence,
  Yet I know by their merry eyes
They are plotting and planning together
  To take me by surprise.

A sudden rush from the stairway,
  A sudden raid from the hall,
By three doors left unguarded
  They enter my castle wall.

They climb up into my turret
  O'er the arms and back of my chair;
If I try to escape, they surround me;
  They seem to be everywhere.

They almost devour me with kisses,
  Their arms about me entwine,
Till I think of the Bishop of Bingen
  In his Mouse-Tower on the Rhine!

Do you think, O blue-eyed banditti,
  Because you have scaled the wall,
Such an old mustache as I am
  Is not a match for you all!

I have you fast in my fortress
  And will not let you depart,
But put you down into the dungeon
  In the round-tower of my heart.

And there will I keep you forever,
  Yes, forever and a day,
Till the walls shall crumble to ruin,
  And moulder in dust away!

Our Secret World
Joy Belle Burgess

It's just four crooked walls
  and a sloping floor,
With a ladder that leads
  to a squeaky trapdoor,
But to my little boy
  it's a castle on high . . .
A tower of gold
  that touches the sky!

It's a bright citadel
  where he may survey
The green of the hills
  and the blue of the day;
Where he may look out
  from his magical throne
And wonder and dream
  in a world of his own.

It's a fortress strong
  in the highest boughs,
In the maze of green leaves
  and fleecy-white clouds,
Where he may be charmed
  by a butterfly's wings,
A chipmunk that scolds,
  and a bird that sings.

It's just four crooked walls
  and a sloping floor,
With a ladder that leads
  to a squeaky trapdoor.
But to my little boy
  it's a castle on high . . .
A tower of gold
  that touches the sky!

©

The Tree House
Peggy Mlcuch

The tree house was our kingdom and
  The storehouse of our dreams;
'Twas here we planned our days of fun
  And built delightful schemes.

The tree house was our secret world
  Where grown-ups could not go;
Where childish fun and fantasy
  Might ever freely flow.

©

A Place To Dream

Patricia Mongeau

Did you ever build a tree house
On a sunny day in spring,
High up in the treetops
Where the happy robins sing?

I built a tree house long ago,
High in a big oak tree,
And there I used to sit and dream
While robins sang to me.

When gentle summer breezes
Swayed the branches to-and-fro,
The robins sang sweet melodies
In tones so soft and low.

That big oak tree still stands today,
Though the tree house is not there.
But if you look up high, you'll see
A birdhouse resting there.

And as the breezes gently
Sway the branches of the tree,
You'll hear the robins singing
A happy melody!

©

Growing Up

Kay Stillwell

There once was a time
　Which is hard to recall,
When high was a bird
　And round was a ball.

When long was an hour
　And big was a tree,
And there wasn't a thing
　More important than me.

Now high is in light years
　And round is the world,
Now long is eternity's
　Ages unfurled.

Now big is the universe
　Dwarfing our sky . . .
I think everything's growing
　Much faster than I.

©

Sea Memories

Henry Wadsworth Longfellow

Often I think of the beautiful town
That is seated by the sea;
Often in thought go up and down
The pleasant streets of that dear old town,
    And my youth comes back to me.
    And a verse of a Lapland song
    Is haunting my memory still:
    "A boy's will is the wind's will,
And the thoughts of youth are long, long thoughts."

I can see the shadowy lines of its trees,
And catch, in sudden gleams,
The sheen of the far-surrounding seas,
And the islands that were the Hesperides
    Of all my boyish dreams.
    And the burden of that old song,
    It murmurs and whispers still:
    "A boy's will is the wind's will,
And the thoughts of youth are long, long thoughts."

I remember the black wharves and the ships,
And the sea tides tossing free;
And the Spanish sailors with bearded lips,
And the beauty and mystery of the ships,
    And the magic of the sea.
    And the voice of that wayward song
    Is singing and saying still:
    "A boy's will is the wind's will,
And the thoughts of youth are long, long thoughts."

The Mariner

John C. Evans

In my window seat I rock and sway;
I am the ship's lookout today,
And watching from my crow's nest here,
I'll wait till lunch and peek and peer.

For hours the great winds, wild and free,
Have roared across this stretch of sea,
And so I'm sharp and quick to spy
The vessels that go racing by.

My white sails bulge and crack and blow
On the long clothesline out below.
And thundering ships that wallow hard
Are the white hens blown about the yard.

The huge waves crash and surge and pass
Across the long, high meadow grass.
And so I'll sit and watch the sea
Till Mother comes and calls for me.

©

Two Angels Live At Our House

Jeanne Karnes Driver

Two angels live at our house!
Though you may think this odd,
I guess they are ambassadors
Sent to our house from God.

They don't resemble angels
In the most accepted way . . .
No harps, no wings, no halos,
Nor heavenly array.

No classic noble features,
They each have upturned nose,
And jelly on their chubby cheeks;
And usually their clothes

Bear evidence of mud pies
Or a telltale fence post rip,
And their little unseen halos
Occasionally slip!

They shout and become noisy,
They often slam the doors,

Eat cookies by the dozen,
And try to skip their chores.

The noise and dirt and freckles
Are misleading, I'll admit,
And yet I know they're angels,
They're not fooling me a bit.

A hundred things betray them
In spite of their disguise:
I see their angel innocence
Illumined in their eyes.

I hear it in their voices sweet
Each time they say a prayer.
I feel it in their kisses.
Oh, so often I'm aware
Of the magic charm of heaven
Compressed in miniature . . .

And I feel God's warmth about us,
And that's why I'm so sure
That two angels live at our house!

I Believe In Little Ones

Garnett Ann Schultz

I believe in little ones, with laughter
    soft and sweet,
In little hearts so full of love, to make
    our lives complete;
So much of happiness they lend, so much
    that's real and true,
A little girl, a little boy, a world of
    gladness too.

*I believe in little smiles, what gladnesses
    they bring,
In little voices gay and proud, a little
    song to sing,
A tender kiss upon my cheek, a hug that
    warms my heart,
A little child so full of life, with
    heaven to impart.*

I believe in little dreams and little
    thoughts to share,
In all the precious little ways that life
    will banish care.
A youngster is a tender jewel with beauty
    so ideal,
And I believe in little ones, with love and
    gladness real.

*I believe in little ones, in little stars
    that shine,
In each tomorrow God shall send, to thrill
    this heart of mine;
The children that He lends us all, to have,
    to love, to share . . .
I do believe in little ones He places in
    our care.*

©

THE IDEALS OBSERVER

Hometown, U.S.A.

Editor's Column of Old Favorites
THE SHIP OF STATE
Henry Wadsworth Longfellow

Thou, too, sail on, O ship of State!
Sail on, O Union, strong and great!
Humanity with all its fears,
With all its hopes of future years,
Is hanging breathless on thy fate!
We know what Master laid thy keel,
What workmen wrought thy ribs
  of steel,
Who made each mast, and sail,
  and rope,
What anvils rang, what hammers
  beat,
In what a forge and what a heat
Were shaped the anchors of thy
  hope!
Fear not each sudden sound and
  shock,
'Tis of the wave and not the rock;
'Tis but the flapping of the sail,
And not a rent made by the gale!
In spite of rock and tempest's roar,
In spite of false lights on the shore,
Sail on, nor fear to breast the sea!
Our hearts, our hopes, are all with
  thee,
Our hearts, our hopes, our prayers,
  our tears,
Our faith, triumphant o'er our
  fears,
Are all with thee,—are all with
  thee!

INVICTUS
William Ernest Henley

Out of the night that covers me,
Black as the Pit from pole to pole,
I thank whatever gods may be
For my unconquerable soul.

In the fell clutch of circumstance
I have not winced nor cried aloud.
Under the bludgeonings of chance
My head is bloody, but unbowed.

Beyond this place of wrath and
  tears
Looms but the horror of the shade,
And yet the menace of the years
Finds and shall find me unafraid.

It matters not how straight the
  gate,
How charged with punishments
  the scroll,
I am the master of my fate:
I am the captain of my soul.

From POEMS by William Ernest Henley
(Charles Scribner's Sons)

A PSALM OF LIFE
Henry Wadsworth Longfellow

Tell me not, in mournful numbers,
Life is but an empty dream!—
For the soul is dead that slumbers,
And things are not what they
  seem.

Life is real! Life is earnest!
And the grave is not its goal;
Dust thou art, to dust returnest,
Was not spoken of the soul.

Not enjoyment, and not sorrow,
Is our destined end or way;
But to act, that each tomorrow
Find us farther than today.

Art is long, and Time is fleeting,
And our hearts, though stout
  and brave
Still, like muffled drums, are
  beating
Funeral marches to the grave.

In the world's broad field of battle,
In the bivouac of life,
Be not like dumb, driven cattle!
Be a hero in the strife!

Trust no Future, howe'er pleasant!
Let the dead Past bury its dead!
Act,—act in the living Present!
Heart within, and God o'erhead!

Lives of great men all remind us
We can make our lives sublime,
And, departing, leave behind us
Footprints on the sands of time;

Footprints, that perhaps another,
Sailing o'er life's solemn main,
A forlorn and shipwrecked brother,
Seeing, shall take heart again.

Let us, then, be up and doing,
With a heart for any fate;
Still achieving, still pursuing,
Learn to labor and to wait.

REQUIEM
Robert Louis Stevenson

Under the wide and starry sky
Dig the grave and let me lie;
Glad did I live and gladly die,
And I laid me down with a will.

This be the verse you grave for me;
Here he lies where he longed to be;
Home is the sailor, home from sea,
And the hunter home from the hill.

From UNDERWOODS by Robert Louis Stevenson
(Charles Scribner's Sons)

BE THE BEST OF WHATEVER YOU ARE
Douglas Malloch

If you can't be a pine on the top of
  the hill,
Be a scrub in the valley—but be
The best little scrub by the side of
  the rill;
Be a bush if you can't be a tree.

If you can't be a bush, be a bit of
  the grass,
Some highway happier make;
If you can't be a muskie, then just
  be a bass—
But the liveliest bass in the lake!

We can't all be captains, we've got
  to be crew,
There's something for all of us
  here,
There's big work to do, and there's
  lesser to do,
And the task we must do is the
  near.

If you can't be a highway, then
  just be a trail,
If you can't be the sun, be a star;
It isn't by size that you win or
  you fail—
Be the best of whatever you are!

THE AMERICAN'S CREED
William Tyler Page

I believe in the United States of
  America as a government of the
  people, by the people, for the
  people;
Whose just powers are derived
  from the consent of the
  governed;
A democracy in a republic, a
  sovereign nation of many
  sovereign states;
A perfect union one and in-
  separable;
Established upon those principles
  of freedom, equality, justice,
  and humanity for which American patriots sacrificed their lives
  and fortunes.
I therefore believe it is my duty to
  my country to love it, to support
  its Constitution, to obey its laws,
  to respect its flag, and to defend
  it against all enemies.

COLUMBUS
Joaquin Miller

Behind him lay the gray Azores,
Behind the Gates of Hercules;
Before him not the ghost of
  shores;
Before him only shoreless seas.
The good mate said: "Now must
  we pray,
For lo! the very stars are gone.
Brave Admiral, speak, what shall
  I say?"
"Why, say, 'Sail on! sail on!
  and on!' "

"My men grow mutinous day by
  day;
My men grow ghastly wan and
  weak."
The stout mate thought of home;
  a spray
Of salt wave washed his swarthy
  cheek.
"What shall I say, brave Admiral,
  say,
If we sight naught but seas at
  dawn?"
"Why, you shall say at break of
  day:
'Sail on! sail on! sail on! and on!' "

They sailed and sailed, as winds
  might blow,
Until at last the blanched mate
  said:
"Why, now not even God would
  know
Should I and all my men fall dead.
These very winds forget their way,
For God from these dread seas is
  gone.
Now speak, brave Admiral, speak
  and say—"
He said: "Sail on! sail on! and on!"

They sailed. They sailed. Then
  spake the mate:
"This mad sea shows his teeth
  tonight.
He curls his lip, he lies in wait,
With lifted teeth, as if to bite!
Brave Admiral, say but one good
  word:
What shall we do when hope is
  gone?"
The words leapt like a leaping
  sword:
"Sail on! sail on! sail on! and on!"

Then pale and worn, he kept his
  deck,
And peered through darkness. Ah,
  that night
Of all dark nights! And then a
  speck—
A light! A light! A light! A light!
It grew, a starlit flag unfurled!
It grew to be Time's burst of
  dawn.
He gained a world; he gave that
  world
Its grandest lesson: "On! sail on!"

*From SELECTIONS FROM THE
POEMS OF JOAQUIN MILLER
by Juanita Joaquina Miller*

I WANDERED LONELY AS A CLOUD
William Wordsworth

I wandered lonely as a cloud
That floats on high o'er vales and
  hills,
When all at once I saw a crowd,
A host, of golden daffodils;
Beside the lake, beneath the trees,
Fluttering and dancing in the
  breeze.

Continuous as the stars that shine
And twinkle in the Milky Way,
They stretched in never-ending line
Along the margin of a bay:
Ten thousand saw I at a glance,
Tossing their heads in sprightly
  dance.

The waves beside them danced;
  but they
Out-did the sparkling waves in
  glee:
A poet could not but be gay,
In such a jocund company:
I gazed—and gazed—but little
  thought
What wealth the show to me had
  brought:

For oft, when on my couch I lie
In vacant or in pensive mood,
They flash upon that inward eye
Which is the bliss of solitude;
And then my heart with pleasure
  fills,
And dances with the daffodils.

THE GATE OF THE YEAR
M. Louise Haskins

And I said to the man who stood
  at the gate of the year:
"Give me a light, that I may tread
  safely into the unknown."
And he replied:
"Go out into the darkness and put
  your hand into the Hand of God.
That shall be to you better than
  light and safer than a known
  way."
So, I went forth, and finding the
  Hand of God, trod gladly into
  the night.
And he led me towards the hills
  and the breaking of the day in
  the lone East.
So, heart, be still:
What need our little life,
Our human life, to know,
  If God hath comprehension?
In all the dizzy strife
Of things both high and low
  God hideth His intention.

*From THE TREASURE CHEST
By Permission of Harper & Row Publishers*

O CAPTAIN! MY CAPTAIN!
Walt Whitman

O Captain! my Captain! our fear-
  ful trip is done,
The ship has weathered every rack,
  the prize we sought is won,
The port is near, the bells I hear,
  the people all exulting,
While follow eyes the steady keel,
  the vessel grim and daring;
But O heart! heart! heart! O the
  bleeding drops of red,
Where on the deck my Captain lies,
  Fallen cold and dead.

O Captain! my Captain! rise up
  and hear the bells;
Rise up—for you the flag is flung—
  for you the bugle trills,
For you bouquets and ribboned
  wreaths—for you the shores a-
  crowding,
For you they call, the swaying
  mass, their eager faces turning;
Here Captain! dear father!
  This arm beneath your head!
It is some dream that on the deck
  You've fallen cold and dead.

My Captain does not answer, his
  lips are pale and still,
My father does not feel my arm, he
  has no pulse nor will,
The ship is anchored safe and
  sound, its voyage closed and
  done,
From fearful trip the victor ship
  comes in with object won;
Exult O shores, and ring O bells!
  But I with mournful tread,
Walk the deck my Captain lies,
  Fallen cold and dead.

CROSSING THE BAR
Alfred, Lord Tennyson

Sunset and evening star,
And one clear call for me!
And may there be no moaning of
  the bar
When I put out to sea.

But such a tide as moving seems
  asleep,
Too full for sound and foam,
When that which drew from out
  the boundless deep
Turns again home.

Twilight and evening bell,
And after that the dark!
And may there be no sadness of
  farewell
When I embark.

For tho' from out our bourne of
  Time and Place
The flood may bear me far,
I hope to see my Pilot face to face
When I have crost the bar.

BATTLE HYMN OF THE REPUBLIC
Julia Ward Howe

Mine eyes have seen the glory of
the coming of the Lord:
He is trampling out the vintage
where the grapes of wrath are
stored;
He hath loosed the fateful lightning
of His terrible swift sword:
His truth is marching on.

I have seen Him in the watch-fires
of a hundred circling camps,
They have builded Him an altar in
the evening dews and damps;
I can read His righteous sentence
by the dim and flaring lamps:
His day is marching on.

I have read a fiery gospel, writ in
burnished rows of steel:
"As ye deal with my contemners,
so with you my grace shall deal;
Let the Hero, born of woman,
crush the serpent with His heel,
Since God is marching on."

He has sounded forth the trumpet
that shall never call retreat;
He is sifting out the hearts of men
before His judgment seat.
Oh, be swift, my soul, to answer
Him! be jubilant, my feet!
Our God is marching on.

In the beauty of the lilies Christ
was born across the sea;
With a glory in His bosom that
transfigures you and me;
As He died to make men holy, let
us die to make men free,
While God is marching on.

TREES
Joyce Kilmer

I think that I shall never see
A poem lovely as a tree.

A tree whose hungry mouth is
prest
Against the earth's sweet flowing
breast;

A tree that looks at God all day
And lifts her leafy arms to pray;

A tree that may in summer wear
A nest of robins in her hair;

Upon whose bosom snow has lain;
Who intimately lives with rain.

Poems are made by fools like me,
But only God can make a tree.

IT COULDN'T BE DONE
Edgar A. Guest

Somebody said that it couldn't be
done,
But he with a chuckle replied
That "maybe it couldn't," but he
would be one
Who wouldn't say so till he'd tried.
So he buckled right in with the
trace of a grin
On his face. If he worried he hid it.
He started to sing as he tackled
the thing
That couldn't be done, and he
did it.

Somebody scoffed: "Oh, you'll
never do that;
At least no one ever has done it";
But he took off his coat and he
took off his hat,
And the first thing we knew he'd
begun it.
With a lift of his chin and a bit
of a grin,
Without any doubting or quiddit,
He started to sing as he tackled
the thing
That couldn't be done, and he
did it.

There are thousands to tell you it
cannot be done,
There are thousands to prophesy
failure;
There are thousands to point out
to you, one by one,
The dangers that wait to assail you.
But just buckle in with a bit of a
grin,
Just take off your coat and go to it;
Just start to sing as you tackle
the thing
That "cannot be done," and
you'll do it.

A CREED
Edwin Markham

There is a destiny that makes us
brothers;
None goes his way alone:
All that we send into the lives of
others
Comes back into our own.

I care not what his temples or his
creeds,
One thing holds firm and fast—
That into his fateful heap of days
and deeds
The soul of man is cast.

L'ENVOI
Rudyard Kipling

When Earth's last picture is
painted, and the tubes are
twisted and dried,
When the oldest colors have faded,
and the youngest critic has died,
We shall rest, and, faith, we shall
need it—lie down for an eon
or two,
Till the Master of All Good Workmen shall set us to work anew!

And those that were good shall be
happy: they shall sit in a golden
chair;
They shall splash at a ten-league
canvas with brushes of comets'
hair;
They shall find real saints to draw
from—Magdalene, Peter, and
Paul;
They shall work for an age at a
sitting and never be tired at all!

And only the Master shall praise
us, and only the Master shall
blame;
And no one shall work for money,
and no one shall work for fame;
But each for the joy of the working, and each, in his separate
star
Shall draw the Thing as he sees It
for the God of Things as They
Are!

OLD IRONSIDES
Oliver Wendell Holmes

Ay, tear her tattered ensign down!
Long has it waved on high,
And many an eye has danced to see
That banner in the sky;
Beneath it rung the battle-shout,
And burst the cannon's roar:
The meteor of the ocean air
Shall sweep the clouds no more!

Her deck, once red with heroes'
blood,
Where knelt the vanquished foe,
When winds were hurrying o'er
the flood
And waves were white below,
No more shall feel the victor's
tread,
Or know the conquered knee:
The harpies of the shore shall pluck
The eagle of the sea!

O better that her shattered hulk
Should sink beneath the wave!
Her thunders shook the mighty
deep,
And there should be her grave:
Nail to the mast her holy flag,
Set every threadbare sail,
And give her to the god of storms,
The lightning and the gale!

I Remember

Eleanor Lyons Culver

I remember when a nickel was a fortune
   in my pocket
To be spent for penny candy at the store.
There were rows of tempting goodies to entrance
   an eager child . . .
Oh, on earth, could any mortal ask for more!

I remember the piano that we'd sit and pump
   for hours,
And the taffy pulls we often would enjoy;
Games of authors, picture puzzles, and those
   other family projects
That made life happy for each girl and boy.

I remember pets we cherished, cats and fuzzy
   little puppies;
There were always one or two about the place.
I remember friends we played with, fought and argued
   and made up with . . .
Vividly I see each dear familiar face.

I remember, I remember . . . how the thoughts come
   flooding through me!
Let me turn aside awhile to sit and gaze
At the pictures that are bound within the album
   of my memory,
As I call to mind the joy of other days.

©

What Is a Boy?

Alan Beck

Between the innocence of babyhood and the dignity of manhood we find a delightful creature called a boy. Boys come in assorted sizes, weights, and colors, but all boys have the same creed: To enjoy every second of every minute of every hour of every day and to protest with noise (their only weapon) when their last minute is finished and the adult males pack them off to bed at night.

Boys are found everywhere—on top of, underneath, inside of, climbing on, swinging from, running around, or jumping to. Mothers love them, little girls hate them, older sisters and brothers tolerate them, adults ignore them, and Heaven protects them. A boy is Truth with dirt on its face, Beauty with a cut on its finger, Wisdom with bubble gum in its hair, and the Hope of the future with a frog in its pocket.

When you are busy, a boy is an inconsiderate, bothersome, intruding jangle of noise. When you want him to make a good impression, his brain turns to jelly or else he becomes a savage, sadistic, jungle creature bent on destroying the world and himself with it.

A boy is a composite—he has the appetite of a horse, the digestion of a sword swallower, the energy of a pocket-size atomic bomb, the curiosity of a cat, the lungs of a dictator, the imagination of a Paul Bunyan, the shyness of a violet, the audacity of a steel trap, the enthusiasm of a firecracker, and when he makes something he has five thumbs on each hand.

He likes ice cream, knives, saws, Christmas, comic books, the boy across the street, woods, water (in its natural habitat), large animals, Dad, trains, Saturday mornings, and fire engines. He is not much for Sunday School, company, schools, books without pictures, music lessons, neckties, barbers, girls, overcoats, adults, or bedtime.

Nobody else is so early to rise, or so late to supper. Nobody else gets so much fun out of trees, dogs, and breezes. Nobody else can cram into one pocket a rusty knife, a half-eaten apple, 3 feet of string, an empty Bull Durham sack, 2 gum drops, 6 cents, a slingshot, a chunk of unknown substance, and a genuine supersonic code ring with a secret compartment.

A boy is a magical creature—you can lock him out of your workshop, but you can't lock him out of your heart. You can get him out of your study, but you can't get him out of your mind. Might as well give up—he is your captor, your jailer, your boss, and your master—a freckled-face, pint-sized, cat-chasing, bundle of noise. But when you come home at night with only the shattered pieces of your hopes and dreams, he can mend them like new with two magic words—"Hi Dad!"

What Is a Girl?

Alan Beck

Little girls are the nicest things that happen to people. They are born with a little bit of angel-shine about them, and though it wears thin sometimes, there is always enough left to lasso your heart—even when they are sitting in the mud, or crying temperamental tears, or parading up the street in Mother's best clothes.

A little girl can be sweeter (and badder) oftener than anyone else in the world. She can jitter around, and stomp, and make funny noises that frazzle your nerves, yet just when you open your mouth, she stands there demure with that special look in her eyes. A girl is Innocence playing in the mud, Beauty standing on its head, and Motherhood dragging a doll by the foot.

Girls are available in five colors—black, white, red, yellow, or brown—yet Mother Nature always manages to select your favorite color when you place your order. They disprove the law of supply and demand—there are millions of little girls, but each is as precious as rubies.

God borrows from many creatures to make a little girl. He uses the song of a bird, the squeal of a pig, the stubbornness of a mule, the antics of a monkey, the spryness of a grasshopper, the curiosity of a cat, the speed of a gazelle, the slyness of a fox, the softness of a kitten, and to top it all off He adds the mysterious mind of a woman.

A little girl likes new shoes, party dresses, small animals, first grade, noisemakers, the girl next door, dolls, make-believe, dancing lessons, ice cream, kitchens, coloring books, make-up, cans of water, going visiting, tea parties, and one boy. She doesn't care so much for visitors, boys in general, large dogs, hand-me-downs, straight chairs, vegetables, snowsuits, or staying in the front yard. She is loudest when you are thinking, the prettiest when she has provoked you, the busiest at bedtime, the quietest when you want to show her off, and the most flirtatious when she absolutely must not get the best of you again.

Who else can cause you more grief, joy, irritation, satisfaction, embarrassment, and genuine delight than this combination of Eve, Salome, and Florence Nightingale? She can muss up your home, your hair, and your dignity—spend your money, your time, and your temper—then just when your patience is ready to crack, her sunshine peeks through and you've lost again.

Yes, she is a nerve-racking nuisance, just a noisy bundle of mischief. But when your dreams tumble down and the world is a mess—when it seems you are pretty much of a fool after all—she can make you a king when she climbs on your knee and whispers, "I love you best of all!"

The Homey Things

Wilma Harper

There's something about the homey things,
Something real and fine . . .
Of geraniums in a window box,
A snowy wash upon the line;

Of fresh-baked rolls and gingerbread,
And sparkling dishes in a row;
Of fluffy towels and fresh-mopped floors
And a broad sunbonnet of calico.

There's something about these homey things
That ravels out the knot of care,
And warms the heart with loveliness,
Then leaves a calm contentment there.

©

The Sweetest Place

Mamie Ozburn Odum

The sweetest place in the wide, wide world
. . . Is home at the end of the day . . . Here
there is peace beyond compare . . . And
rest comes in to stay . . . Home is the place
where hearts find peace . . . Here there is
happiness and play . . . Here love and
honor binds family ties . . . And one forgets
the hard long day . . . Home is the sacred
place we love . . . Here we build our hopes
with pride . . . And our children bind us
closely . . . From morn till eventide . . .
Home is the place hard to describe . . . A
father's prayer . . . A mother's kiss . . .
Seek far and near the wide world o'er . . .
There is no other place like this.

©

OLD-FASHIONED REFLECTIONS

Laurie English Dawson

Potbellied stoves and warm cozy rooms,
Sturdy geraniums with gay crimson blooms.

A fire to sit by and read or just dream,
A kitchen with windows for watching moonbeams.

Calico dresses with big swirling skirts,
Sunbonnets, suspenders and stiff-collared shirts.

Horses and buggies, a pony and saddle,
A hillside and pasture to graze sheep and cattle.

Nut hunting and fishing with worms and a pole,
The sheer joy of plunging in a cold swimming hole.

A rocker, a cradle, a fat feather bed,
To lull into slumber each small sleepyhead.

Sunflowers and corncribs, bobsleds and mittens,
Haylofts and hen nests and warm furry kittens.

Box suppers and pie salads, cakewalks so gay,
Ice cream from a freezer at the end of the day.

Bread baking and canning on the big kitchen range,
Fresh eggs for the huckster for notions exchange.

Molasses and cider, both milled in their season,
And having a picnic for no certain reason.

Hayrides and corn popping, I like to recall
Old-fashioned memories are best of them all.

©

MY COPY OF "IDEALS"

Naomi I. Parks

Today I watched the postman
As he came along the walk,
I met him on the doorstep
For our little morning talk;
We spoke about the weather,
How the nights were growing chill,
The new folks on the corner,
An old friend who was ill.

He handed me some letters
And a folder with no seal,
Then a neatly wrapped brown parcel
With my copy of "IDEALS".
I thanked him most sincerely,
Went inside and closed the door;
Forgot the breakfast dishes,
And the crumbs upon the floor.

I put the letters on the table,
Curled up in my favorite nook,
Left this world and found another
In the pages of my book.
With care and thought I read
Each lovely illustrated poem,
Wandered through the springtime beauty
To a real old-fashioned home.

I know that there are others
Who would think my time ill-spent,
For instead of doing housework
Here I sat in sweet content.
But the treasures that I gathered
Were a priceless, golden store
Of peace and true thanksgiving
In my heart forevermore.

©

Catalog of Beauty

Nadine Delling Garner

In wonder I behold them,
The works that Thou hast made;
The glory of the sunshine,
The restfulness of shade;

The proud heights of the mountain,
The valley's modest flower,
The white of endless desert,
The green of woodland bower;

The mystery of weather,
The changes seasons bring;
The smoky haze of autumn,
The clear perfume of spring;

All nature's perfect patterns . . .
The milkweed's down-filled case,
The insect's iridescent wing,
The spider's fragile lace;

The light of priceless diamonds,
Gay lamps of fireflies,
The planets in the heavens and
The light in children's eyes;

The song of birds at dawning,
The crimson close of day,
The magic touch of moonbeams
Across the silent bay.

Oh, beauty, beauty, beauty!
Such wonders never cease.
And what is man, dear Father,
To merit gifts like these?

©

A Faded Rose

Juanita Johnson

While searching through the attic,
I chanced to find one day
A diary from a bygone age,
Tucked carefully away.

*It was not so much the diary
That set my heart aglow,
But the thing I found inside it,
A faded yellow rose . . .*

A rose plucked from a bride's bouquet
And pressed tween pages there;
The petals crisp and falling now,
Held memories so dear.

*With trembling hand, I touched the rose,
As tears fell where it lay,
And for a fleeting moment
I recaptured yesterday.*

As trembling lips repeated vows
We made so long ago,
My heart was glad that I had found
That faded yellow rose.

*And I rushed forth rebuilding dreams
That time had slowly waned,
Thanking God for a faded rose . . .
And love refreshed again.*

Accumulation

Author Unknown

As one accumulates old things,
And multiplies his store
Until the crowded attic room
Cannot hold any more,

*So does the heart keep gathering
Treasures along the way,
Till it is full of this and that
From many a yesterday.*

Petals of mem'ry brown and dead,
Moments that throbbed and thrilled,
The unforgotten touch of hands,
Voices that one day filled

*Our little world with happiness,
Words spoken in the glow
Of some lost twilight in the spring,
And songs of long ago.*

Old-Fashioned Things

Josephine Millard

I tiptoe up the creaking stairs
And gently slip into the gloom,
Where all my treasures lie secure
Within that little attic room.

I wipe away the dust with care
From each dear thing that quickly brings
A memory from long ago
On shadow-soft and silent wings.

I sit awhile and try to grasp
Each lovely dream all edged in gold;
I seek to find that faith complete,
A bit of yesterday to hold.

Why does my heart so often crave
Old-fashioned things from out the past,
Old-fashioned things that seem to hold
The kind of goodness that will last?

Why do I find such tranquil peace
Among my treasures old and rare?
Why does my day seem more complete
When I have climbed that creaking stair?

©

Attic Conspiracy

Shirley Sallay

One chore that comes each springtime
That I don't mind at all,
Is cleaning out the attic
Beneath the rafters tall.

Of course, there's very little
That I ever throw away,
But each year I make a pretense
Of straightening the disarray,

Somehow before I know it
I've found a cozy chair,
And a box of old-time pictures,
Or a faded teddy bear,

Souvenirs and trinkets,
All bound to memory;
A trunk of Mother's dresses
Or booties she made for me.

The hours pass like minutes,
Cleaning tools are brushed aside,
As I recall fond yesterdays
With sentimental pride.

A baby spoon of silver,
A china cup for tea,
A humidor of Grandpa's
Are all a conspiracy

To keep me from the task at hand.
It's just as if they know
That I could never part with them,
Or the dreams that they bestow.

©

Lovely Things Are Silent

Lovely things are silent . . .
Rosebuds waxing bloom,
Shadows stealing softly
In a darkened room;
Dragonflies on rushes,
Stars in dark blue skies;
Hatching, fuzzy birdlets,
Love in sweethearts' eyes.

Lovely things are silent . . .
Rainbows in the sky,
Violets shedding fragrance,
A soft breeze waltzing by;
An apple tree in blossom,
Sunsets all aglow;
Moonlight on the water,
Falling soft white snow.

Lovely things are silent . . .
Foam clouds in the sky,
Hummingbirds at flowers,
Butterflies gliding by.
A spider's dainty spinning,
Wild flowers on a hill.
I bow my head in silence
And in my heart I'm still.

© Betty Fox Solberg

I Am a Tree

Nancy Corinne Zuelch

I am a tree . . .
   gnarled, twisted, bent;
Growth straight and tall was my intent
But wind-whipped gales
   from a storm-tossed sea
Battered my branches relentlessly.
No beauty of stature or form I claim . . .
Homely, rugged, bleak and plain.
But deep within the heart of me
Is strength born of adversity.

Man, whipped by gales of deep despair,
Of woe and sorrow, worry, care,
May carry scars that do not show
And cover wounds only they can know . . .
But look within and we may see
A strength born of adversity.

©

My Little Green Valleys

Myrtle Van Campen

I call them my little green valleys,
All the beautiful places I've seen.
They hang in my heart's art gallery,
Life refreshing, as oases green.

When the pressures of life seem heavy
And take on a shade of blue,
I open the door to my treasures
And view them for a moment or two.

Once again I am in a green valley,
Or climbing a high mountain trail;
Playing on oceans' white beaches
Or cruising a lake in full sail.

When life's blessed strength is waning,
And too much leisure has come my way,
I will still have my little green valleys
To distract the monotony of day.

I thank God for the little green valleys
That should be in everyone's heart.
They are sweet balm to dull, tired living . . .
Priceless pieces of natural art.

©

The Brood

Old Mother Robin is bursting with song,
Chirping her love notes all the day long;
Hovering over her green leafy nest,
Bringing the morsels her babies like best.

Deep in the branches she cradles her young,
Troubling not over storm clouds or sun;
Cheerfully tending her brood in the nest,
Grateful for guidance from One who knows best.

The Flight

Gaily she twitters instructions to fly
Over the meadow and through the blue sky;
Leaving their nest for the first thrilling flight
Through the deep shadows and into the light.

Never recalling the brood to the nest,
Old Mother Robin leaves shelter and rest;
Winging her way through the soft summer air,
Trusting her fledglings to God's tender care.

© Vivian A. McCormick

Painting opposite
ROBIN AND HER YOUNG
by Harry J. Moeller

Square Dance Tonight

Ruth B. Field

Down through the meadow,
Just over the hill,
And turn to the left by
The old gristmill.

*Follow your nose, then
Soon you'll see the light
Of lanterns shining on the sign:
"Square Dance Tonight."*

Now choose your partner
As fiddles loudly sing.
Bow to the ladies and
Swing, boys, swing!

*Sashay down the center,
And now do-si-do,
(Steal just a little kiss
Where the lights are low.)*

Portland Fancy, Plain Quadrille,
Stay where you are,
Sailors' Delight, Money Musk,
And the Morning Star.

*Eight hands around, folks . . .
Watch it, don't fall.
Make the rafters shake and ring,
Then promenade, all.*

©

Barn Dance

Mildred L. Potts

The Saturday night barn dances
Gathered folks from far and near.
The caller's voice for square dancing,
Rang out very loud and clear.

The best of the peppy music
Which musicians played so loud
Erased tired and weary feelings
For the happy merry crowd.

Young and old sat on the sideline,
Clapping hands and tapping feet
As the dancers swung their bodies
In a tempo with the beat.

Maidens' skirts were gay and ruffled,
And men donned bright colors too.
It was a brilliant fiesta
For all who gazed at the view.

The musicians seemed to profit
From such a picturesque crowd,
And furnished tunes appropriate,
Though competition was loud.

Saturday night at a barn dance
Is so much fun to attend,
For it leaves a glorious feeling
Which one wishes would never end.

©

H. MOELLER

Spring Gossip

Lola Taylor Hemphill

The birds were house hunting in your yard
   the other day,
And I overheard them gossip in a noisy sort
   of way.
"Now, the wrens may have the lilac hedge
   for their nest so round and small,
And the orioles pin their hanging nest
   in the swaying willow tall.

The peach tree holds the catbird's home
   and the little cherry tree
Seems just the proper leafy spot for the thrush
   to live, you see.
The cedar tree that hugs the house, where it's cool
   and dark alway,
The cardinals have chosen for their concert
   everyday.

Out in the honeysuckle bush, where the blossoms
   pink are spread,
Are the very lovely grosbeaks with their throats
   of rosy red.
The blackbirds built down by the lake,
   the elm is for the jays,
But oh! we have the maple for our happy
   summer days

Where we will build the nicest nest for our eggs
   of robin blue
And trill our music skyward when every day
   is new.
Our tree is strong and tall and wide,
   but here's the nicest thing . . .
It shades a lovely sandpile, and a little child's
   rope swing."

©

The Changing Times

John Packham

I think of days that have gone by when mother
  baked her bread.
Back in those days one didn't buy but made
  such things instead.
I could smell the rich aroma from the oven
  that was hot,
And I'll not forget the homemade bread that
  Dad and I once got.
There was something in its flavor, in its added
  bit of zest,
That made you feel, beyond a doubt, that homemade
  bread was best.

*But times have changed. The women folks no
  longer seem to bake.*
*They buy from stores that stock the things
  commercial bakers make.*
*The cakes and pies and other things no longer
  have the touch*
*Of homemade things that man once said he liked
  so very much.*
*Those good old days when homemade bread was
  wholesome, fresh, and plain*
*Will far outlive these things today all wrapped
  in cellophane.*

Yes, times have changed. And in a way I think
  that it is best.
The woman who once baked her bread has now more
  time to rest.
She need not watch an oven with an ever-watchful eye;
All this has passed and now belongs to days that
  have gone by.
But I, for one, remember and I've more than often said
The better days were back in days when man had
  homemade bread.

Bread

Kathryn Boice

"Give us this day our daily bread,"
I fold my hands and bow my head,
And through my prayer-closed eyes I see
The miracle of bread for me.

The fallow loam neath winter snow,
Green tender shoots, row after row,
That climb through wind to meet the rain;
The majesty of waving grain
With heads held high to summer sun.
The golden copper of each one
That falls before the shining knife
To bring to me the staff of life.

In bread I see the tiring toil
Of harvest hands, the sweat, the soil,
The dust, the noise, machines that roar
Above the shouts of men. No more
Will I break bread alone . . . I share
My loaf with the hungry everywhere.

Speaking of Flowers

Maurice Allen

I wonder who painted the orchid with colors
    of perfect hue?
I wonder who blended the pigment, and whose
    was the hand that drew
The pattern of fragile beauty where the soul
    of a flower might dwell.
I wonder whose hand was the artist's . . .
    If only a flower could tell.

I wonder who painted the orchid and whose
    was the hand that made
From the dust of the earth this beauty,
    Though every bloom must fade.
I still shall remember the image, the vision
    that never dies . . .
The flame and the purple of sunset, the soul
    of the western skies.

©

From the Editor's Scrapbook

1

Home is the place where character is built, where sacrifices to contribute to the happiness of others are made, and where love has taken up its abode.

Elijah Kellogg

2

Be resolutely and faithfully what you are; be humbly what you aspire to be. Man's noblest gift to man is sincerity, for it embraces his integrity also.

Thoreau

3

4

8

When one door closes, another opens; but we often look so long and so regretfully upon the closed door that we do not see the one which has opened for us.

Alexander Graham Bell

9

10

Give me your tired, your poor, your huddled masses yearning to breathe free. The wretched refuse of your teeming shore, send these; the homeless, tempest-tossed to me. I lift the lamp beside the golden door.

Emma Lazarus
Inscription on the Statue of Liberty

11

15

16

The heights by great men reached and kept were not attained by sudden flight, but they, while their companions slept, were toiling upward in the night.

Longfellow

17

A good book is the best of friends . . . the same today and forever.

Tupper

The flower that follows the sun does so even on cloudy days.

Leighton

18

22

Never in history have so many owed so much to so few.

Winston Churchill

They are never alone who are accompanied by noble thoughts.

Sir Philip Sidney

23

24

That which is past and gone is irrevocable: wise men have enough to do with things present, and to come.

Francis Bacon

Success is never final and failure never fatal. It's courage that counts.

George F. Tilton

25

29

As long as I live, I'll hear waterfalls and birds and winds sing. I'll interpret the rocks, learn the language of flood, storm and avalanche. I'll acquaint myself with the glaciers and wild gardens, and get as near the heart of the world as I can.

John Muir

30

God always gives us strength to bear our troubles day by day; but He never calculated on our piling the troubles past, and those to come, on top of those of today.

Elbert Hubbard

5

Blessed is that person who has found his niche in life and is happy in filling it.

Elmer R. Horne

Do the duty which lieth nearest to thee! Thy second duty will already have become clearer.

Thomas Carlyle

6

7

To be happy is not the purpose of our being, but to deserve happiness.

Fichte

In doing what we ought we deserve no praise, because it is our duty.

St. Augustine

12

I remember, I remember,
The house where I was born . . .
The little window where the sun
Came peeping in at morn.

Thomas Hood

Though we travel the world over to find the beautiful, we must carry it with us or we find it not.

Author Unknown

13

There is no top!
No matter how high we rise,
We discover infinite distances above.

Parlette

Where there is an open mind there will always be a frontier.

Charles F. Kettering

14

19

20

He is great who inspires others to think for themselves.

Elbert Hubbard

Through the beauties of nature and growing things one sees the everlasting presence of God.

L. Leota Holland-Damon

21

In an active life is sown the seed of wisdom; but he who reflects not, never reaps.

Edward Young

He who labors diligently need never despair; for all things are accomplished by diligence and labor.

Menandes

26

Who has seen the wind?
Neither you nor I:
But when the trees bow down their heads,
The wind is passing by.

Christina Rossetti

27

28

Days that are past are gone forever, and those that are to come may not come to you; therefore, enjoy the present without regretting the loss of what has past, or depending too much on that which is not yet here. This instant is yours; the next still belongs to futurity, and you do not know what it may bring forth.

Dandemis

Yellow Flowers

Bertha Gerneaux Woods

The painted cups, the pitcher plants,
The rock-set columbines that dance
With every breeze, the gentian's blue,
Joe Pye weed's lovely, old rose hue,
The bloodroot, the anemone,
Each carries thoughts of God to me.

But somehow in the golden things
Each season prodigally brings,
I find Him most to meet my need.
The cowslip and the jewel-weed,
The buttercup, wood betony . . .
Each brings Him very near to me.

Who has not felt his throat grow tense
When on some zigzag country fence
He glimpses trailing bittersweet?
Who has not walked with reverent feet
Through paths made bright by goldenrod,
And breathed a voiceless "Thank you, God"?

Our sincere thanks to the author
whose address we were unable to locate.

Wondering

Agnes Davenport Bond

Were you lonesome, mountain cabin,
When your roof was piled with snow?
When no cheerful fire was burning
With its leaping, ruddy glow?

Did the clock upon the cupboard
Stop its friendly ticking then?
Did the squirrels and blue jays leave you,
Scamper to their wooded glen?

Did the whistling winds of winter,
Some weird stories to you tell,
As they rustled through the treetops,
While the snowflakes thickly fell?

Tell me truly, mountain cabin,
Are you glad the spring is here,
With the breath of flowers about you
And the tumbling brook so near?

Are you glad to hear our footsteps,
Glad the porch is cleared of snow . . .
Glad to see the ones who love you?
Tell me, I would like to know.

©

Quiet Interlude

Hilda Butler Farr

There is a need for quietness
In everybody's day,
Sometimes it's difficult to find
Within life's frenzied fray.

*The moments spent alone can be
A haven for the soul,
A time for rich replenishment
To help one reach his goal.*

How often one must search for time
In which to meditate,
The days when it's impossible
And one is forced to wait.

*But when the opportunity
Arrives, how blessed indeed
Becomes the quiet interlude
We all so deeply need.*

©

A Little Bit

Mamie Ozburn Odum

There's a little bit of heaven
In the evening's softened gloam,
And a joyous happy feeling
In the place we call our home.

There's a little bit of heaven
In the sunlit skies at dawn,
And the wild birds' blended anthem,
And a graceful, leaping fawn.

There's a little bit of heaven
In a zigzag fence of rails,
And the mystery of silence
In lone winding forest trails.

There's a little bit of heaven
In baby eyes and cunning smile,
The soft feel of arms a-clinging,
Free of deceit and of guile.

There's a little bit of heaven
In a rosebud kissed by dew,
In moonlight skies and cooling rain
And rest when day is through.

There's a little bit of heaven
In the coming of a new day;
And the heart fills with thanksgiving
For each gift along the way.

©

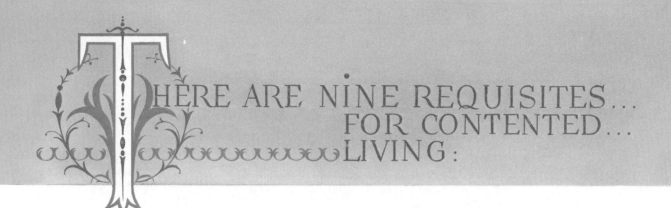

THERE ARE NINE REQUISITES...
FOR CONTENTED...
LIVING:

Health enough to make work a pleasure;

Wealth enough to support your needs;

Strength enough to battle with difficulties
and overcome them;

Grace enough to confess your sins
and forsake them;

Patience enough to toil until some good
is accomplished;

Charity enough to see some good
in your neighbor;

Love enough to move you to be useful
and helpful to others;

Faith enough to make real the things
of God;

Hope enough to remove all anxious fears
concerning the future.

GOETHE

Only $1.75
Cellophaned
Art Cover

RUSTIC IDEALS

he magnificence of the American countryside, the wonders of
ature, and the simple but important expressions of home,
iendship, love, neighborliness set in a theme of rustic beauty
.. and the nostalgic days of earlier years.

addition to single copy purchases, enrich the lives of those
ou love with a year round IDEALS gift subscription. A lovely
ft announcement will be sent to the recipient of your gift sub-
ription heralding your thoughtfulness and good wishes.

or birthdays, wedding anniversaries, for that special remem-
rance for the shut-in . . . for any occasion when a meaningful
ft is needed, select the IDEALS way to remember friends and
ved ones.

You are invited to enter a subscription to *ideals*

You can enjoy wholesome and inspiring reading
the year round by entering a subscription to
IDEALS, the most beautiful book published in
America today.

Whether you select OLD FASHIONED IDEALS—
or RUSTIC IDEALS as the first issue on your subscription, you enjoy the holidays and seasons of
the year in a more meaningful, exciting way as
they are beautifully portrayed for you in IDEALS.

So distinctly refreshing . . . filled with inspiring
words of nostalgic thoughts, IDEALS truly reflects wholesome, clean, old-fashioned American
thoughts and ideals.

Each page of IDEALS is beautiful enough to
frame. Reproductions of the world's finest art—
of both the old masters and contemporary artists
as well—are featured in full natural colors. Outstanding and brilliant photographic reproductions are so vivid you'll feel a special excitement
as you view them in IDEALS.

The words of gifted writers and poets are ex-
quisitely illustrated, to create for you a tranquil
mood and peace of mind so often lost in these
busy and troubled times.

An IDEALS subscription brings a new beautiful
issue into the home once every 60 days. Colorfully illustrated and artistically presented, IDEALS
contains no advertising.

1969-1970 Schedule

RUSTIC IDEALS . . . . July 1969

HARVEST IDEALS . . . . Sept. 1969

CHRISTMAS IDEALS . . . . Nov. 1969

INSPIRATION IDEALS . . . . Jan. 1970

EASTER IDEALS . . . . March 1970

Ideals Subscription Plans

ONE YEAR   6 issues as published   only $ 7.50
A SAVING OF $3.00 OVER THE SINGLE COPY PRICE.
TWO YEARS   12 issues as published   only $14.00
A SAVING OF $7.00 OVER THE SINGLE COPY PRICE.
FOUR VOLUMES   4 issues as published   only $ 5.00
A SAVING OF $2.00 OVER THE SINGLE COPY PRICE.

★

PAY-AS-YOU-READ one copy each issue as published   only $ 1.50
—a reserve copy will be sent AUTOMATICALLY with an   per copy
invoice for $1.50.
A 25c SAVING OVER SINGLE COPY PRICE

A Delightful Gift Today, A Remembrance Forever

God's Beautiful World

What finer remembrance gift than a lovely book that reflects God's masterful hand in the creation of the natural beauty which surrounds us. In GOD'S BEAUTIFUL WORLD, God is found in the mountains . . . the woodlands . . . the sea . . . in the simplest flower . . . and in all things bright and beautiful.

Colorfully illustrated poems . . . inspiring art . . . full color photographic reproductions convey a tranquility to mind—a sense of contentment—so needed in our busy troubled world today.

For all occasions . . . for all those you love and hold dear, GOD'S BEAUTIFUL WORLD is a delightful year round gift book remembrance . . . especially appropriate as a gift for Mom on her special day, Sunday May 11th.

Actual Size 5⅜ x 7¼ inches
Colorful Hard Bound Book
52 pages

Only $2.00 *each*

Flowers of Friendship

The meaningful words of gifted writers express beautifully the true meaning of friendship. "Our Friendship"—"Friends Are Like Flowers"—"Friendship's Perfect Gift"—are but a few of the lovely poems reflecting the strong bond that is friendship.

Vividly colorful photographic reproductions of familiar flowers form the delightful backgrounds in this unusual gift book. As each lovely page unfolds, the colorful freshness of roses, daffodils, daisies, petunias and other familiar flowers portray the beauty and warmth of friendship.

An appropriate Mother's Day gift—and as a year round expression of thoughtfulness, FLOWERS OF FRIENDSHIP is a lasting and never to be forgotten friendship gift.

Coffee Break

Now content with our true friendship,
Far away from duty's call,
We will sip our cup of coffee . . .
This the brightest hour of all.

Jessie Cannon Eldridge

Portfolio of Art Prints

Print size
8½ by 11 inches

Only $1.00 each set of fou

Captivating, delightful, these colorful reproductions have been selected especially for another new IDEALS Portfolio of Prints.

The talents of outstanding pet photographers are vividly displayed in this lovely set of color reproductions—suitable for framing. As separate single framed prints or in a group arrangement, each colorful print will add a special brightness to your home.

For distinctive gift giving, each set is beautifully packaged in a window portfolio as pictured on the left. Order Set #16 Cat Prints.

A Special Birthday Wish

BIRTHDAY SIGNS

An unusual but most distinctive and interesting birthday greeting that says, "Here is my wish for your birthday. May your dreams come true and I hope you'll find pleasure in reading what the stars have to say about you."

Each sign of the zodiac is presented in full color page reproductions from original paintings by the talented artist, Frans Van Lamsweerde.

Dramatically illustrated, the meaning of each zodiac sign throughout the year is expressed through appropriate poem and prose.

A delightful way to say Happy Birthday.

Only 60¢ each with greeting card envelope
Booklet size 5⅜ x 7¼ inches
Cellophane art covers

My Personal Order

YOUR NAME _____ Please print clearly

ADDRESS _____

CITY _____

STATE _____ ( ) _____ *ZIP CODE

IMPORTANT

1. Items checked below will be sent directly to you at the address to the left.

2. Enter gift orders in the space provided in the area below marked "MY GIFT ORDER."

3. Please tally your entire order and enter it in the space provided on the reverse side.

Beautiful Ideals Issues

QUANTITY	TITLE	PRICE		QUANTITY	TITLE	PRICE
	OLD FASHIONED IDEALS 1969	@ $1.75			HEARTHSIDE IDEALS 1968	@ $1.75
	RUSTIC IDEALS 1969	@ $1.75			SCENIC IDEALS 1967	@ $1.75
	REFLECTION IDEALS 1969	@ $1.75			CHRISTMAS IDEALS 1968	@ $1.75
	VACATION IDEALS 1968	@ $1.75			THANKSGIVING IDEALS 1968	@ $1.75
	HOMETOWN IDEALS 1968	@ $1.75			CHRISTMAS IDEALS 1966	@ $1.75

PLEASE PRINT IN ADDITIONAL ITEMS BELOW

Ideals Subscription Plans

CHECK ✓	SUBSCRIPTIONS WILL BEGIN WITH ISSUE MARKED			CHECK STARTING ISSUE	
	4 VOLUME SUBSCRIPTION (4 CONSECUTIVE ISSUES)	@ $5.00	BEGIN ☐ OLD FASHIONED IDEALS 1969	☐ RUSTIC IDEALS 1969	
	ONE YEAR (6 CONSECUTIVE ISSUES)	@ $7.50	BEGIN ☐ OLD FASHIONED IDEALS 1969	☐ RUSTIC IDEALS 1969	
	TWO YEAR (12 CONSECUTIVE ISSUES)	@ $14.00	BEGIN ☐ OLD FASHIONED IDEALS 1969	☐ RUSTIC IDEALS 1969	
	PAY-AS-YOU READ 1 COPY EACH ISSUE WITH INVOICE	@ $1.50	BEGIN ☐ OLD FASHIONED IDEALS 1969	☐ RUSTIC IDEALS 1969	

My Gift Order

GIFT NAME _____ Please Print Clearly

ADDRESS _____

CITY _____

STATE _____ ( ) _____ *ZIP CODE

Identify As A Gift

From _____

*Please indicate zip code in order that we may process and deliver this order as rapidly as possible.

Beautiful Ideals Issues

QUANTITY	TITLE	PRICE		QUANTITY	TITLE	PRICE
	OLD FASHIONED IDEALS 1969	@ $1.75			HEARTHSIDE IDEALS 1968	@ $1.75
	RUSTIC IDEALS 1969	@ $1.75			SCENIC IDEALS 1967	@ $1.75
	REFLECTION IDEALS 1969	@ $1.75			CHRISTMAS IDEALS 1968	@ $1.75
	VACATION IDEALS 1968	@ $1.75			THANKSGIVING IDEALS 1968	@ $1.75
	HOMETOWN IDEALS 1968	@ $1.75			CHRISTMAS IDEALS 1966	@ $1.75

PLEASE PRINT IN ADDITIONAL ITEMS BELOW

Ideals Subscription Plans

CHECK ✓	SUBSCRIPTIONS WILL BEGIN WITH ISSUE MARKED			CHECK STARTING ISSUE	
	4 VOLUME SUBSCRIPTION (4 CONSECUTIVE ISSUES)	@ $5.00	BEGIN ☐ OLD FASHIONED IDEALS 1969	☐ RUSTIC IDEALS 1969	
	ONE YEAR (6 CONSECUTIVE ISSUES)	@ $7.50	BEGIN ☐ OLD FASHIONED IDEALS 1969	☐ RUSTIC IDEALS 1969	
	TWO YEAR (12 CONSECUTIVE ISSUES)	@ $14.00	BEGIN ☐ OLD FASHIONED IDEALS 1969	☐ RUSTIC IDEALS 1969	

If you have friends or relatives who would be interested in receiving a catalog of Ideals Publications, please list their names below.

NAME _____ Please print clearly

ADDRESS _____

CITY _____

STATE _____ ( ) _____ ZIP CODE

NAME _____ Please print clearly

ADDRESS _____

CITY _____

STATE _____ ( ) _____ ZIP CODE

In order to process and deliver your order as rapidly as possible . . . Please write or type your proper Zip Code in the space provided. The Postal Department soon will make Zip Codes mandatory on all mailing addresses.

*YOUR ZIP CODE IS NECESSARY

SEAL WELL and MAIL

Check or Money Orders May Be Enclosed with Safety

Important Note—

The Postal Authorities strongly recommend that you send your remittance by check or money order.

AFTER you have entered and checked your entire order in the spaces provided — please tally your order here to assure accuracy of your remittance.

If you desire additional gift copies or subscriptions sent to your friends attach a separate list and they will be handled promptly and carefully for you.

FOLD HERE FIRST

FOLD SIDE FLAPS FIRST — THEN FOLD HERE

from

ZIP CODE

ideals PUBLISHING CO.
P.O. BOX 1101
MILWAUKEE, WIS. 53201

FOLD HERE FIRST

When properly sealed with the above gummed flap this envelope and its contents will travel safely through the mail.

FOREIGN POSTAGE ONLY

***FOREIGN POSTAGE
EXCEPT U.S. AND POSSESSIONS
CANADA AND MEXICO**

Four Volume Subscription	Add $ .60
One Year Subscription	Add $1.00
Two Year Subscription	Add $2.00
IDEALS Binder	Add $ .50
Single IDEALS	Add $ .15
Each Single Hardbound Book	Add $ .15
Each Set of Prints	Add $ .14
Gift Book	Add $ .20
Calendars	Add $ .14

QUANTITY	TITLE		AMOUNT
	4 Volume Subscription	@ $5.00	
	1 Year Subscription	@ $7.50	
	2 Year Subscription	@ $14.00	
	IDEALS Issues	@ $1.75	
	IDEALS Binder	@ $3.00	
	Greeting Card Booklets	@ 60¢	
	Hardbound Books	@ $1.75	
	Gift Books	@ $2.00	
	Birthday Calendars	@ $1.00	
	Prints	@ $1.00	
	*Foreign Postage		

*Add Foreign Postage Where Applicable   I Enclose My ☐ Check ☐ Money Order
[Canada Currency Exchange — Add 7% to Total]
No additional postage for U.S. mailings.